Backyard Animals
Raccoons

Jennifer Hurtig

Weigl Publishers Inc.

Published by Weigl Publishers Inc.
350 5th Avenue, Suite 3304, PMB 6G
New York, NY 10118-0069
Website: www.weigl.com

599.76
qhurtig

Library of Congress Cataloging-in-Publication Data

Hurtig, Jennifer.
  Raccoons / Jennifer Hurtig.
     p. cm. -- (Backyard animals)
  ISBN 978-1-59036-669-1 (hard cover : alk. paper) -- ISBN 978-1-59036-670-7 (soft
cover : alk. paper)
  1. Raccoons--Juvenile literature. I. Title.
  QL737.C26H87 2008
  599.76'32--dc22
                                        2006102018

Printed in the United States of America
1 2 3 4 5 6 7 8 9 0 11 10 09 08 07

Editor Heather C. Hudak
Design and Layout Terry Paulhus

Cover: Raccoons live all over North, Central, and South America. In North America,
raccoons have adapted well to living near humans.

Contents

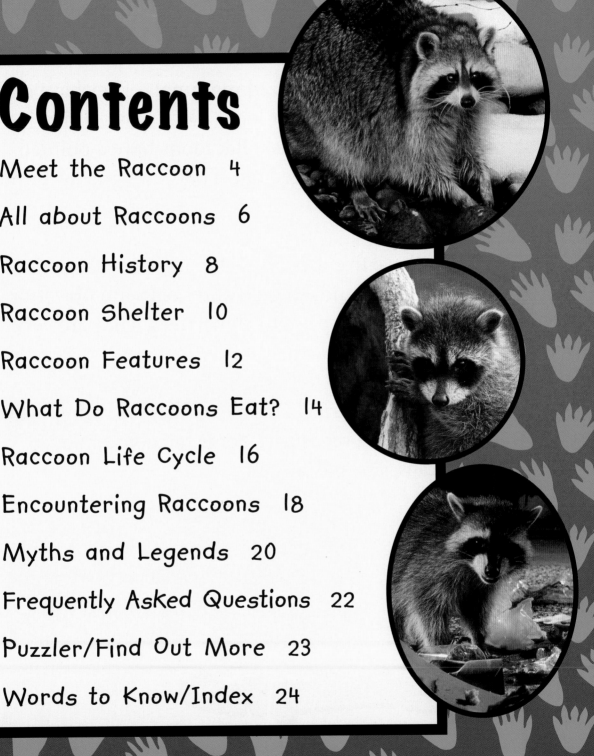

Meet the Raccoon

Raccoons are medium-sized **mammals**. They have dark fur around their eyes that looks like a mask. There is white fur around the mask. Raccoons have a pointed snout and a bushy, ringed tail. They have gray or brown fur on their body.

Raccoons have five toes on each paw. They use their front paws like hands to grab and hold onto objects. Raccoons use their paws to climb trees. They are very good swimmers.

Raccoons are nocturnal. This means they are mainly active at night. They are very smart. Some raccoons can open garbage cans, jars, and latches.

Raccoons can climb down trees headfirst. They do this by turning their hind feet so that their toes face backwards.

Baby raccoons live and travel with their family for up to one year before living on their own.

All about Raccoons

Raccoons belong to a group of tree-climbing mammals. This group is closely related to bears.

There are seven **species** of raccoons. They live in North, South, and Central America. Each place offers different food, climates, and **habitats**. Some types of raccoons are rare and are not found easily by people.

Raccoons search for food in streams. They use their paws to turn over rocks and small tree branches.

Where Raccoons Live

Bahaman Raccoon	Cozumel Island Raccoon
• Lives in the Bahamas	• Found on Mexico's Cozumel Island

Barbados Raccoon	Crab-eating Raccoon
• Once lived in the Barbados • The last one seen by humans was in 1964	• Lives in marshy and jungle areas in Central and South America

Common Raccoon

• Lives in Canada, United States, and South America	• Often lives near humans

Guadeloupe Raccoon	Tres Marias Raccoon
• Lives on the Caribbean island of Guadeloupe	• Found on the Tres Marias Islands, near Mexico

Raccoon History

Little is known about when raccoons first appeared on Earth. Some people believe that early American Indians hunted raccoons for food and fur. Later, they traded raccoon pelts with Europeans.

Many settlers began to hunt raccoons. They wore "coonskin" hats that were made of raccoon fur. In the 1920s, raccoon skin coats became popular. Today, some people still hunt raccoons for their fur.

Sometimes raccoons are trapped because they ruin farmers' crops. Raccoons also are threatened by a lack of food sources, **predators**, and diseases such as rabies.

Raccoons communicate with each other by chirping, growling, crying, or hissing.

Raccoons are native to North and South America. People have brought them to live in Europe and Asia.

Raccoon Shelter

Raccoons can be found in cities and towns. They live near trees and water. Most raccoons do not make their own homes. They live in buildings, hollow tree trunks, old nests, wood piles, hay stacks, or under objects. They may live in beaver lodges and coyote or badger dens that have been left empty.

Raccoons live in different climates. Some live in hot and humid forests. Others live farther north where the weather is colder. A raccoon that lives in a cold place has thicker fur than one that lives in a warm place.

Raccoons are not active in winter. They stay in dens for long periods of time when it is cold. In warm weather, raccoons lay on the ground or on tree branches.

Raccoons move to a new living space every few days, except when they are breeding or taking care of their young.

Raccoon Features

Raccoons have **adapted** to living in many different habitats. Thick fur keeps them warm in winter. The color of their fur helps them hide from predators because it blends with their surroundings. Their toes and claws allow them to hold items such as food. Other parts of a raccoon's body have special features as well.

EARS AND EYES
Raccoons have excellent night vision and good hearing.

FEET
A raccoon's foot has claws on each of its five toes. Raccoons can spread their toes to grab food and other objects.

FUR

Raccoons have long fur that most often is a brownish-gray color. The darker fur around their eyes may help them to see better at night. It helps reduce the glare of the Sun and the Moon.

TAIL

A raccoon's tail fur usually has five to seven dark circles. Raccoons use their tail for balance when they are climbing.

LEGS

A raccoon's back legs are longer than its front legs. Raccoons cannot run very fast. They waddle when they walk. However, they can swim and climb trees.

What Do Raccoons Eat?

Raccoons are **omnivores**. They eat insects, birds, eggs, fish, and young rabbits. They also eat fruits and vegetables, such as plums and corn. Near water, raccoons hunt for crayfish. They look for insects under rocks. Raccoons dig in gardens and pick at food in bird feeders.

The food raccoons eat changes with the seasons. In spring, raccoons mainly eat meat. In summer, they eat berries, nuts, and other plants. In autumn, raccoons eat more food than they do at other times of the year. They do this to prepare for winter. Raccoons eat corn, nuts, and grain to build fat. They use the fat reserves to survive in cold weather when food is more difficult to find. During this time, up to half of the raccoon's body weight may be fat.

The scientific name for raccoons is *Procyon Lotor*. This means "washer bear." Raccoons earned this name because they often dip their food in water.

Raccoons have long canine teeth that they use to eat meat. Raccoons also have strong molars that they use to eat other foods, such as fruits.

Raccoon Life Cycle

Most raccoons look for a mate in January or February. The mother will give birth about 63 days later. Raccoons that live in northern areas will have three to seven babies. In southern places, female raccoons have two to three babies. Baby raccoons are called cubs or kits.

Baby

A baby raccoon weighs less than 3 ounces (85 grams) when it is born. A raccoon cub's eyes do not open until a few weeks later. At birth, a cub's fur is light gray. It darkens in the following weeks. The mask appears when the cub is about 10 days old.

1 Month Old

At one month of age, a raccoon cub weighs 10 to 16 ounces (283 to 454 g). It can stand up. When cubs are two to three months old, they begin to hunt with their mother. She protects them from predators. Most raccoons stay with their mother for up to one year.

A female raccoon may stay with her **litter** until she has another one. Males live alone. They do not help raise the babies.

Adult

Adult raccoons can grow to be 3 feet (0.9 meter) long. Most raccoons weigh about 30 pounds (14 kilograms), but some can be almost 40 pounds (18 kg). Male raccoons are usually bigger than females. In nature, raccoons live for about five to eight years.

Encountering Raccoons

Sometimes raccoons live near people. They can cause damage to gardens and spill trash cans. If a raccoon lives near your home, do not feed the animal. It is better to urge the raccoon to move to another place. Raccoons prefer to look for food in the dark. Turning on lights will annoy the raccoon.

People should not keep raccoons as pets. They often become **aggressive** as they age. If they are released into nature, they will not have the skills they need to survive.

Raccoons can get **parasites** and diseases such as roundworm or rabies. They can pass on these diseases to pets and humans.

Useful Websites

To learn more about caring for raccoons, visit:
www.raccoonrescue.com

Raccoons that live near people may search through garbage cans for food.

Myths and Legends

Stories and legends about raccoons often show the tricky side of this clever animal. Raccoons are curious animals. This sometimes leads them into trouble. Many American Indian legends describe the raccoon as a mischief maker that plays tricks on other animals and people.

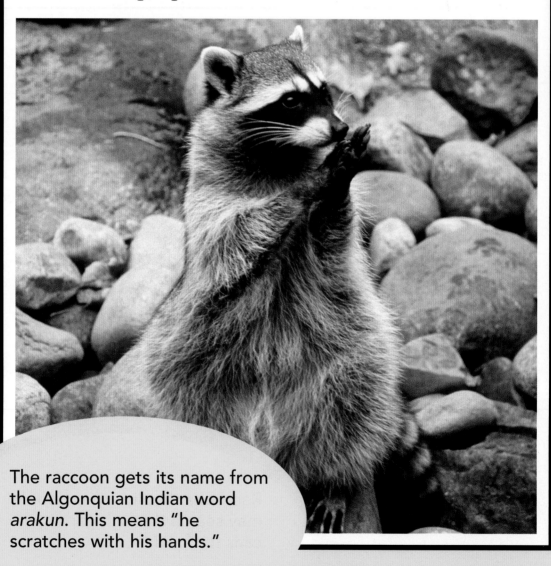

The raccoon gets its name from the Algonquian Indian word *arakun.* This means "he scratches with his hands."

The Raccoon and the Blind Men

A version of this legend is part of many American Indian cultures.

Two old, blind men lived together. One day, they were cooking eight pieces of meat, four for each of them. The men each took one piece of meat to eat. A raccoon passing by decided to play a trick on the old men. He quietly picked out four pieces of cooked meat. Then one of the men put his hand in the bowl to take another piece of meat. He found that there were only two pieces left. "My friend," he said to the other old man, "you must be very hungry to have gobbled up so much meat already."

The other replied, "I have not taken it. I think you have eaten it yourself." The two men began to argue. Raccoon was watching them, and he began to laugh. Then he took the last two pieces of meat and left. Raccoon called back to the men.

"I have played a trick on you. You should not blame each other so easily."

Frequently Asked Questions

Why do raccoons climb inside garbage cans?

Answer: Raccoons are very curious. They enjoy climbing and crawling into small places. They search garbage cans for food because sometimes they cannot find enough food in nature.

How do raccoons spend the winter?

Answer: Raccoons are not active in winter. They mainly stay in their den. They use up their fat when they cannot find food.

What should I do if I find an ill raccoon?

Answer: If you find an ill raccoon, you should call a veterinarian, or animal doctor, for help. Do not to touch the animal.

Puzzler

See how much you know about raccoons.

1. How many different species of raccoons are there?
2. Why are raccoons hunted?
3. What do raccoons eat?
4. How many toes does a raccoon have?
5. What are baby raccoons called?

Answers: 1. seven 2. for their fur and meat 3. crayfish, fruit, vegetables, fish, insects, and birds 4. 20 total, 5 on each foot 5. cubs or kits

Find Out More

There are many more interesting facts to learn about raccoons. Look for these books at your library so you can learn more.

MacClintock, Dorcas. *A Natural History of Raccoons.* Blackburn Press, 2003.

Sullivan, Pat Harvey. *Raccoons and their Relatives.* World Book, 2002.

Words to Know

adapted: adjusted to the natural environment

aggressive: to behave in an unfriendly manner

habitats: natural environments of living things

litter: a group of animals born to one mother at the same time

mammals: animals that have warm blood and feed milk to their young

omnivores: animals that eat meat and plants

parasites: living things that live on or in other living things

predators: animals that hunt other animals for food

species: a group of animals that share specific features

Index